A STEP BY STEP
HOUSEBREAKING
YOUR PUPPY

JACK C. HARRIS

Photography: Isabelle Francais, Ron Reagan, Vince Serbin. Humorous drawings by Andrew Predimano.

We at TFH Publications and the above photographers are especially grateful to the following owners for their cooperation in supplying models for this text: Akita, pp. 5,8, Edward Israel, Windom Akitas; Basenji, p. 29, Karen Jenkins and Margret Gougelman; Basset Hound, pp. 7, 9, Howard Nygood; Boxer, p. 31, Richard Tomita; Bulldog, p.15, Vernon and Karen Norris of Richmond, VA; Cardigan Welsh Corgi, p.35, Paul Slaboda; German Short-haired Pointer, p.33, Michael Zollo, agent; Standard Schnauzer, pp. 22, 47, Hanaraan; p. 34, Georgia and Sue Baines, agents and handlers.

Distributed in the UNITED STATES by T.F.H. Publications, Inc., One T.F.H. Plaza, Neptune City, NJ 07753; in CANADA to the Pet Trade by H & L Pet Supplies Inc., 27 Kingston Crescent, Kitchener, Ontario N2B 2T6; Rolf C. Hagen Ltd., 3225 Sartelon Street, Montreal 382 Quebec; in CANADA to the Book Trade by Macmillan of Canada (A Division of Canada Publishing Corporation), 164 Commander Boulevard, Agincourt, Ontario M1S 3C7; in ENGLAND by T.F.H. Publications Limited, Cliveden House/Priors Way/Bray, Maidenhead, Berkshire SL6 2HP, England; in AUSTRALIA AND THE SOUTH PACIFIC by T.F.H. (Australia) Pty. Ltd., Box 149, Brookvale 2100 N.S.W., Australia; in NEW ZEALAND by Ross Haines & Son, Ltd., 18 Monmouth Street, Grey Lynn, Auckland 2, New Zealand; in the PHILIPPINES by Bio-Research, 5 Lippay Street, San Lorenzo Village, Makati Rizal; in SOUTH AFRICA by Multipet Pty. Ltd., 30 Turners Avenue, Durban 4001. Published by T.F.H. Publications, Inc. Manufactured in the United States of America by T.F.H. Publications, Inc.

CONTENTS

INTRODUCTION

"A dog is man's best friend." The origin of this time-honored statement is unknown, but millions of dog lovers throughout the world believe that its basic truth cannot be disputed. However, a great number of them may waver from this resolve if their beloved pet has not been properly housebroken. If not conducted with love, patience, and care, housebreaking a dog can be a frustrating, irritating, and maddening experience for both dog and owner. Nothing can spoil a loving relationship between dog and master faster than the results from improper methods of housebreaking.

Many owners who have successfully housebroken their dog have used different methods. These techniques may have, in some way, utilized a crate, newspapers, dog ports, etc., but they are probably all versions of a small number of accepted techniques. Our goal in writing this book is to examine the most common housebreaking methods and to provide dog owners with an omnibus of housebreaking ideas. There are millions of domesticated dogs in the world and it would be ridiculous to believe that a single method for housebreaking will work for every one. Just as human beings are distinct individuals, so are dogs. Nevertheless, there are a number of tried and true housebreaking methods which have been developed over recent years by experts in the field of dog training.

We have researched these methods and are presenting them in hopes that dog owners will find the one that works best with their pet. If one does not prove effective, then an al-

FACING PAGE: Every dog is an individual, learning, loving, and even misbehaving in his own way; here an Akita pup's curiosity has led him into a flower garden—correction may be pending.

ternate may be applied, or a combination of one or more. This collection may also provide individual owners with a basis for developing a new and unique method all their own. Whichever the case, we are sure that the reader will find valuable information that will help to cement the age-old bond between humans and dogs.

A dog's reputation as "man's best friend" is well-deserved. The loyalty, the companionship, the protection, and the love these friendly animals provide their owners with has been thoroughly documented down through the pages of history. While the joys of owning a dog are many, actually raising the animal from its puppy stage is considered by many experts as one of the most rewarding endeavors a family can undertake. The lessons of responsibility and the intricate workings of nature that can be learned from raising a dog educate and fascinate both young and old. These lessons are remembered for a lifetime by both owner and dog and, in the case of the owner, can be applied to many other aspects of life.

Many canines come complete with the proclivity to chew objects not needing such care; fortunately, such pooch pacifying products as the nylon Nylabone® will help curb such desires by satisfying the dog's inherent need to gnaw.

Dogs practice habits they learn during puppyhood. If your pup demonstrates behavior that you may find unacceptable when he is older, even if you find it cute now, you must correct it immediately. Some may find it difficult to reform so adorable a creature as a puppy, but correction early on saves the inconvenience of having a misbehaved dog in the end.

Regardless of its breed, or in what activity it will spend its life, any dog can present initial problems. Some bark constantly or steal food not meant for them. Others may show hyperactivity and dig through or chew prized articles of furniture. Some are afraid of people or other animals. Some bite. Early proper training can prevent or eliminate many of these problems. Housebreaking is the most important training, since it should be the earliest and the foundation upon which all other training should be built. Experts tell us that while it is impossible to teach a dog to reason, a properly trained dog is often able to be trained to an IQ level of an average ten-year-old child. The many documented reports of heroic dogs acting to save humans in unfamiliar situations such as fires are evidence of dogs' remarkable intelligence.

It is during the housebreaking instruction that the dog will first begin to recognize its owner's voice, looks, and scent. If a dog owner gets through housebreaking successfully, then all other training will be easy in comparison; the basic techniques used in housebreaking a dog can later be applied to teaching it to obey other commands or perform tricks.

Obtaining a dog is easy. Pet shops around the world always have eager puppies in their windows who would be very willing to come home with a dog-lover. Not only that, but the people who run and maintain such establishments will be ready and willing to advise the new dog owner in the matters of training and housebreaking the new pet. These people have a wealth of experience that will be an excellent supplement to the housebreaking methods and techniques discussed here. They will also be able to recommend a veterinarian who can

"Me? Really! You want me!" Selecting a puppy may seem like a difficult decision, when actually it is quite simple, for almost any puppy you select will be more than happy to oblige and prove a worthy pet.

provide quality health care in the form of routine check-ups, inoculations, and prompt medical attention in the case of illness or emergency.

If a pet shop doesn't have the breed of dog that you want, you might consider purchasing a dog from a kennel. Animal shelters are another source of pets.

Of course, all new puppies will require housebreaking. If the dog in question is an older one who has lived with a pre-

Any dog that you bring home to keep is going to require the practice of some preliminary housebreaking procedures; even if fully matured, a new dog should be watched carefully in order to detect any deviation from desired rules of housebroken conduct. If any variance is noted, as was the case with this old guy, you should treat the situation as you would with a new puppy and start from scratch with the crate method.

vious family, he or she may already be housebroken. However, it may be wise not to take the word of the previous owner, as his definition of "housebroken" may not be identical to yours. If, for any reason, other than sickness, your dog defecates or urinates indoors, then it is not housebroken—even if it happens only once in awhile. If your dog is under six months old, then it probably hasn't had the opportunity to learn housebreaking. It may be difficult for some dog-lovers to recognize a problem in housebreaking their own dog. The love and devotion they have for their animal may hide what may appear obvious to others. Remember that housebreaking—in fact, *any* training exercise—will better prepare a dog to face life with humans. The more a dog owner knows about his or her pet, the easier it will be to train the animal to conform to the owner's habits and needs. There does not have to be any conflict. Once successful training and housebreaking have been established between dog and master or mistress, then the lives of all concerned will be

Co-existence, mutually beneficial to both man and dog, implies mutual respect and understanding; the person must respect the dog's need for exercise and affection, and the dog must respect its owner's property.

more stable and the relationship will have room to grow toward mutual love, companionship, and respect.

Dog owners may live in rural areas, the suburbs, or the city. While the housebreaking methods may differ because of your location, there should not be insurmountable difficulty in housebreaking your dog in its environment. Dogs are creatures of habit. If the owner successfully teaches the dog the house rules (for becoming housebroken or for any other aspect of dog training), then those rules will become habitual with the dog as well.

Moving from one location to another should not deter the dog owner. Some may say that "you can't teach an old dog new tricks," but this does not apply to housebreaking. Once it is used to a clean environment, the dog will want it kept that way, whether or not he's been moved from the country to an apartment or vice versa. Housebreaking is not a trick, and once a dog has been trained, he will remember that training for life.

Living in a rural area or suburban area is often an advantage to the dog owner when raising a pup, however, the companionship offered by a canine will surely make up for any additional care required in an urban setting.

Canines are very intelligent; even a young pup will quickly learn what his master's actions signal. For example, this little one has perceived the putting away of his toy, a sign that play-time is over; the disappointment is evident.

Foraging through the foliage in search of hidden toys, this lovely little puppy provides unending joys.

Paper Training

It doesn't matter what variety of dog has to be housebroken—the basics are the same with any breed, male or female. Ideally, housebreaking should start with a puppy of no less than three or four months old. At this age, a dog will have just begun to gain conscious control over the sphincter muscles. These are a band of muscle tissue around the body opening through which waste materials are excreted. In an ideal situation, the dog has become aware of this function because it does not wish to soil its immediate surroundings. Experts who have experimented with or researched housebreaking pups younger than three or four months of age have reported only failure and frustration. A pup *must* be physically ready to learn housebreaking or else it will be confused. If housebreaking is started too early, any additional training will suffer great setbacks. It's a bad way to begin what should be a time of mutual love and understanding.

If done properly and with continual vigilance, housebreaking will not take as long as is often believed. The majority of work should be completed within ten to 14 days. The training should not be considered complete by this time, but the initial stumbling blocks will have been cast aside and owner and dog will be well on their way to a solid relationship. Although it varies, the complete process usually takes about two full months.

FACING PAGE: Routine is essential to elementary training. During the housebreaking period, all activities should revolve around the feeding time. Harmonizing the pup's internal body-clock is only accomplished through routine.

Many experts and dog trainers feel that initially house-breaking a pup to newspapers is the most practical approach, although the method is not without problems and possible set-backs. With the newspaper method, the first step is to teach the puppy that the newspaper is the place on which to "go," rather than the "unpapered" area. The "preferred" area is then slowly and methodically altered to eventually lead the dog out-of-doors. The practicality of this method is most evident to apartment dwellers who frown on trying initially to train their dogs to "go" outside. If they are repeatedly forced to take a puppy down several flights of stairs and into the street, they and the dog both become quickly exhausted. This is especially true since puppies sometimes have to relieve themselves up to a dozen times a day.

Routine is one of the keys to housebreaking, and this applies to all other aspects of a puppy's schedule as well. If the puppy is fed at regular intervals, then, after a very short time, it should be easy to closely predict when it needs to relieve it-

The living quarters of your pup must be kept consistently clean. If a puppy lives in a soiled environment, he will come to believe that such is expected and, even in some cases, desired by his owner. If this idea is allowed to settle in the pup's brain, housebreaking will become an acutely unpleasant experience.

Your pet should always have available a bowl full of fresh, cool water. However, during the primary housebreaking process, it will be necessary to control the times at which your pup may freely drink. Be sure that these times are frequent and allow the pup to drink to his full desire. After such indulgences, a walk must always follow.

self. Experts say it is not good practice to leave a water bowl out for the puppy, since this will disrupt a regular schedule of water intake. Instead, about 30 minutes after feeding the puppy, the water bowl should be made available and the puppy should be allowed to drink its fill. In another half hour the physical pressures should create the urge to go. At this moment, it is time to take the puppy outside. Naturally, every dog and every diet is somewhat different and regularity should not be expected in the puppy's bodily functions. A pup will often have to go at times other than the half-hour after eating and drinking. For overnight, experts recommend not letting the puppy drink any water for at least a couple of hours before the household goes to bed for the night. Just before everyone retires, it is suggested that the puppy be led to the papers and urged (with praise) to go. If the pup goes just prior to the closing

down of the household, it often "holds in" for the entire night before going again, giving its trainer the opportunity to continue the housebreaking routine first thing in the early morning.

Whatever established routine is maintained, it should be primarily designed to meet the dog's needs. While this may be inconvenient to the owner's schedule, it may very likely be necessary to the animal's well-being. Such a schedule need not be rigid, but it should be altered only slightly from day to day in the first weeks of housebreaking. Once the dog has fully matured and once training routines have been firmly established, training the animal to a different schedule should not be difficult. While the puppy is young, however, its schedule should have priority.

The reason for spreading newspapers around the dog's immediate area is simply because it is impratical to watch the dog constantly. Newspapers are inexpensive and easy to discard once soiled.

Next, it is always important to keep the puppy within a specific area, as one can observe the animal more closely. Linoleum or tile floors are the best areas for paper training since they are the easiest to keep clean. Some new dog owners may feel that it is cruel to keep their puppy confined to a small area. However, experts point out that this practice is necessary for housebreaking and, once training is successfully completed, it makes the rest of the dog's life much more pleasant. In addition, a close and comfortable area seems quite natural to a puppy.

The kitchen is often the favorite room for housebreaking puppies since its floor is most commonly linoleum or tile. Once the specific "puppy area" is determined, it should be covered with several layers of newspaper. (Some dog owners cover the entire floor in the beginning.) Once the puppy has relieved itself, the soiled papers should be immediately removed and replaced while praising the puppy.

Every puppy appears to have an inborn need for praise, which is one of the five main rules for training any dog. Since all basic training rules come into play when housebreaking a puppy, it can be said that housebreaking lays the basis for

Paper Training

A linoleum or tiled surface is the preferred base on which to lay the training paper. It has been suggested that the entire surface of the pup's living area be covered, with gradual reductions of the paper being made as the pup comes to grasp the intention of the papered design.

all future training. Praise or a firm-voiced disapproval of a puppy's actions are at the very core of the training process. Praise should always be given in a normal voice. Speaking excitedly or in "baby-talk" will only confuse the puppy.

Dogs recognize their owners by a combination of sight, sound, scent, and instinct. If any of these are altered, the dog will detect it and sometimes become confused. The key is to always speak normally, or, in the instance of scolding, in a firm voice. Many of today's dog trainers feel that praise (and, conversely, scolding) are all the keys dog owners need for disciplining their dog. These experts strongly object to hitting dogs with anything, even the traditionally "acceptable" rolled-up newspaper. It is felt that hitting a puppy "in training" is unnecessary. If housebreaking can be established without physical punishment, then such punishment should not be necessary at any time during the dog's life.

When the puppy goes in the proper place, it should be warmly petted and praised—for example, "Good dog, that's it." If the dog errs, it should be shown the scene of the crime,

scolded and immediately taken for a walk. While it may seem odd to take the dog out after it has obviously relieved itself, the act of taking a walk will re-teach the dog where it is supposed to go.

Rewards of food and affection (such as a pat on the head) are also welcome forms of praise that every young dog enjoys. Some experts feel that food rewards work against training, since the animal begins to think about its next "treat" rather than the training session at hand. It might be better to save food treats (as praise) until after the dog reaches a major housebreaking plateau, such as the move from newspapers to out-of-doors. In a negative sense, the dog can also be trained to perform its act out of fear of punishment. While a dog should be taught that having an indoor "accident" will bring punishment, it is not wise to base the entire training routine on this negative concept. Rewards and praise make for better and more rapid results.

Many pups will need a little reinforcement and reminding. A puppy may make tremendous strides toward that housebreaking finish line, only to slip slightly when you think he is home free. If this happens, a scolding must be given. It is tempting to overlook such a slip on account of his previously fine performance, but few things could be more detrimental to the growth of a completely house-broken animal.

Paper Training

The end result of your diligence and care is a fine friend and protector, a loyal companion who will do all he can to please you for the length of his life. A pet canine adds energy, security, and compassion to any home willing to adopt one of these beautiful animals commonly known as "man's best friend."

Initially, a puppy will respond to the tone of its owner's voice rather than the actual meaning of the words. The vocabulary used for a dog should consist of single-syllable words such as "good," "bad," "go," "stay," "come," etc. These words should be spoken in a tone such that the understanding will be crystal clear. Owners should not say, "bad!" in a calm voice or angrily shout, "good!" These mixed-up inflections will only confuse the animal and make it believe it is receiving praise for a wrongful act or punishment for something it's supposed to be doing.

It is necessary that owners show the dog exactly what they want the animal to do or not to do. Standing over the dog as it deposits waste on the paper and repeating, for example, "Good dog! Paper!" will reinforce that this is what it is supposed to be doing. Leading the puppy to an unpapered area, where it may have had a lapse of memory, and sharply saying, "Bad dog," will remind it what not to do.

The last important rule is not to punish the dog after the "crime" has passed. The only way a dog remembers is by constant repetition. If the owner discovers an accident which occurred some time ago, there may be little use in punishing the dog upon discovery. While the scent will still tell the animal that the mess is its own, it may have long forgotten the act and be confused by any subsequent punishment. While many dog trainers preach that owners have to catch the dog "in the act" for any punishment to be effective in the training procedure, this is actually not the case. Catching puppies in the act is sometimes difficult. Unlike older dogs, puppies do not circle and sniff an area before going. They simply squat. It's an action that a trainer has to learn to look for so as to be ready to transfer the puppy quickly to paper or to the outdoors.

In addition, training can be greatly disturbed if an owner begins to call the dog to come to be punished. If this is done, it won't be long before the dog will refuse to come when called, fearing that it will be facing punishment if it does.

These five rules (correct tone of voice, praise/punishment for performance, direct demonstration of expected actions, punishment only for present and not past accidents, and never calling the dog to come to receive punishment) are the building blocks on which an excellent and rewarding human/dog relationship can be built. If these rules are kept as the basic guide in all training routines, then everything—from housebreaking to tricks—should be easy.

Praising the puppy after each disposal of waste will enhance the dog's belief that what it's doing (and *where*) is right and proper. This should be continued for the first day or two. After that, an "off limits" area should be established. The floor of one area (generally the corner farthest from the door to the outside) should be cleaned and disinfected so that the odor will

Paper Training

Some feel that it is more effective to hold the puppy in their hands while they correct him for a wrong-doing. However, this is not encouraged, for once he is picked up, the pup may associate the correction not with the corresponding act but with being in his master's arms. It is best simply to point out the result of the act which is being corrected and render the appropriate punishment.

not call the animal back to the same spot. This cleaning should be done immediately. If the dog is being trained in a less-frequented area such as a basement, there may be a tendency to wait until the puppy has soiled a number of places before doing one massive clean-up. This is not recommended. If the puppy spends any prolonged amount of time in an area spoiled with its own wastes, it will begin to believe that fouling the area is what the owner is expecting of it. If the idea that a soiled environment is a natural state is allowed to be ingrained in the dog's mind, then training will be all the more difficult.

If the dog understands that going on the newspapers is the proper thing to do, it will seek out an alternate papered area next time. If not, and it uses the same (now unpapered spot), it should be scolded so that it will learn that it has made a mistake. It is very optimistic to hope that a dog will figure this out immediately. It will usually take quite a few accidents and punishments for the puppy to get the idea of what is being

taught. When it does finally understand, it will appear to come as a great revelation to the animal. When it needs to relieve itself, it will suddenly go to the very center area of the clean papers and do so. Often it can actually be observed thinking about and figuring out this action just prior to carrying it out. When this finally occurs, it is time for major praise, and for praise in the form of a treat. Even after this stage of housebreaking is reached, there may be lapses which will warrant punishment. If the owner has dropped his or her vigilance for some reason and the dog soils the bare floor, the animal should be led to the spot and its nose gently directed toward the wetted area. *Never rub the dog's nose in its waste.* The smell alone should be enough of a discomfort for the dog, which will recognize its own scent. It will realize that this is its error and will realize what the punishment is being administered for, even if some time has passed from accident to discovery and punishment. By saying, "No, bad dog!" in a firm voice while showing the dog its mistake, the owner will begin an association in the

All future training will be accomplished much more easily if housebreaking is completed in a firm and orderly manner. Housebreaking lays the foundation for all subsequent training.

Play-time is an extremely important part of the housebreaking process. If possible, such times are best spent out of doors. That way, if the pup urinates, he can be lavishly praised, thus reinforcing the idea of where is the appropriate place to go and thereby helping to speed the housebreaking process along its way.

dog's brain. The dog will begin to associate the stern sound of its owner's voice with an unpleasant memory. Once trained, this tone of voice will continue to startle the dog and trigger this memory. After punishment, it is necessary to place the dog on the paper, even though is has obviously just relieved itself. Doing so will reinforce the dog's training of where he is supposed to go. If the dog is caught in the act, the owner simply needs to carefully lift the dog and set it on the paper. Praise should follow.

After each time, the papered area should grow smaller, leading the puppy closer and closer to the door, eventually to the outdoors. When the dog is old enough to go for walks outside, the owner should lead it to the street or other designated and approved areas and allow the dog time to relieve itself. Again, praise should follow the act.

Alternative Methods

Although the majority of experts recommend paper training as the most popular way of housebreaking a dog, there are other well-respected dog fanciers who are dead against it. They cite some of the common problems such as inadvertently training the dog to go *only* on papers, thereby having it frantically searching for papers, even out-of-doors. They mention the possible problem of making the dog believe that, under specific circumstances, it is okay to eliminate wastes inside (something that housebreaking is trying to end once and for all). These anti-paper training experts suggest housebreaking with a wire crate.

Housebreaking with a wire crate centers upon getting the dog used to a routine and schedule that will teach the animal the proper indoor and outdoor habits. If a schedule is strictly maintained, then the puppy will become accustomed to going at certain times of day and staying in its crate during the rest of the time. By establishing these habits slowly, the dog owner will soon be able to increase the length of time the puppy is allowed out of its crate. Before long, the dog will be able to be trusted anywhere in the house.

The wire-mesh construction may resemble a prison or a pen, but its design allows an even and comforting air flow for the dog and lets the animal see all around. Early confinement in a crate will pay off handsomely in the years to come by giving the owner a completely housebroken animal. The lack of

FACING PAGE: The crate method is a highly effective way to housebreak your pup. Contrary to some criticism that it has received, the crate actually provides the puppy with a sense of security and saves him from many uncomfortable corrections.

Although kept as a group within a single crate as younger puppies, once the housebreaking process is to begin, it is not a good idea to keep more than one pup per crate. This is because all pups learn at their own rate and a slower learner may inhibit the progress of quicker one.

tension between the housebroken dog and its proud owner will be worth a short period of time of the puppy's living in a confined, wire-enclosed area.

There are various designs of wire crates available at local pet stores. Many can be folded and are easy to transport. They also serve as excellent carriers if the puppy has to travel. Many owners save the cost of boarding kennels by taking their animals with them on trips or vacations. There are many motels which permit dogs in rooms if they are kept in a wire crate. The crates will safely prevent the dog from escaping and coming to harm. They actually give the animal a sense of security as it becomes used to the confinement. This sense of security is very important in establishing the basis for much future training.

The size of the crate should be determined by the size of the puppy to be trained. The crate is supposed to provide a *confined* area for the dog and should not be large enough for the puppy to eliminate waste at one end and sleep at the other. If this is allowed, the animal will eventually become used to sleeping near its own waste material, which is exactly what housebreaking is trying to teach the animal *not* to do. If the puppy has room to move around too much in its crate, it will have increased need to eliminate its wastes. The whole function of the crate is to teach the puppy to appreciate cleanliness and reduce its urge to evacuate in its living area.

Scenting something disconcerting, this pup re-entered into his crate to make sure that all is well. Dogs often become attached to their "beds" and will work to keep them just right.

Now that all is well, it is time to return to play.

27

Naturally, dogs grow. A small crate used as a housebreaking tool for a puppy won't be much good as a carrier when the dog grows older and larger. With a wire mesh or some other secured barrier, it is possible to reduce the interior size of the larger crate to create the needed housebreaking dimension. These barriers can easily be removed as the dog becomes larger. Once the dog learns not to soil its immediate environment, then the size of the crate won't matter as far as housebreaking is concerned.

It is not necessary to line the bottom of the wire crate with anything. Papers on the bottom (if the dog had any experience at all with paper training) may appear to be an invitation to urinate. If the owner feels more comfortable allowing the puppy to have a towel in the crate, he must be prepared to immediately remove it if the dog does urinate on it. To leave it for any length of time will defeat housebreaking efforts.

Since the whole idea of the crate is to train the puppy and not make it miserable, having a dog toy in the crate is certainly a good idea. The dog will be happier and more content to stay in the small area.

It is very important that dogs not be permitted to

A crate used for housebreaking can later be used when transporting your dog, provided that the dog has not outgrown the crate. A dog that was housebroken in a crate will be used to such temporary confinement.

Looking for some chow during the off-feeding hours, this Basenji pup has just received a brand new Nylabone®; this healthy treat will satisfy the little guy's need to chew while helping to insure proper tooth formation and growth.

chew on anything they can break or on indigestible things from which they can bite sizeable chunks. Sharp pieces, such as those from a bone which can be broken by a dog, may pierce the intestine wall and kill. Indigestible things which can be bitten off in chunks, such as toys made of rubber compound or cheap plastic, may cause an intestinal stoppage; if not regurgitated, they are certain to bring painful death unless surgery is promptly performed.

The nylon bones, especially those with natural meat and bone fractions added, are probably the most complete, safe, and economical answer to the chewing need. Dogs cannot break them or bite off sizeable chunks; hence, they are completely safe. And being longer lasting than the other things offered for the purpose, they are economical.

There are a great variety of Nylabone® products available that veterinarians recommend as safe and healthy for a dog or puppy to chew on. These Nylabone® Pooch Pacifiers can't splinter, chip, or break off in large chunks; instead, they are frizzled by the dog's chewing action, and this creates a

29

toothbrush-like surface that cleanses the teeth and massages the gums. At the same time, these hard-nylon therapeutic devices channel the dog's tensions and chewing frustration into constructive rather than destructive behavior.

If you want a soft, chewy play toy for your dog or puppy, look for Gumabone® products wherever Nylabone® products are sold. These flexible toys are available in various sizes of bones, balls, knots, and rings (and even a tug toy) designed to provide safe entertainment for you and your dog.

It is not a good idea to feed the dog while it is in the crate. Doing so will only make it need to go out at a time that may not meet with the schedule that the owner is trying to establish. In fact, feeding in general needs to be part of scheduling. No dog should have food available at all times. The same is true with water. Constant eating and drinking will only make the dog frequently need to eliminate its waste. It is recommended that the puppy be fed its food at a time when it can be quickly removed from the crate and taken out. The dog should be limited to 15 minutes to eat, so as to discourage dawdling during mealtime. This will also train it not to be fussy. Given only 15 minutes to eat, the puppy will soon realize that if it does not eat on time, the food will be removed and the meal missed. Once a few meals are missed, the dog will know that it had better eat or it will become very hungry.

If an owner's schedule demands, a bowl of ice cubes can be left in the crate for the dog. This will allow the dog to quench its thirst without taking large gulps of water that will cause it to have to urinate off schedule. Also, the slowly melting ice cubes will make the needed water last longer.

Once housebreaking has been established, owners should always have a bowl of cool, fresh water on hand for the dog since it is vitally necessary for the dog's health. Water is needed for the dog's natural internal cooling system, for its digestion, and for normal and safe bodily excretions.

The establishment of a housebreaking schedule is the next important step. A puppy can control its sphincter muscles for only about eight hours at a stretch. When it is an adult it will be able to spend the night without having to go out. While training, however, owners will have to adjust their schedules to

From puppyhood through maturity, a canine's need to chew is strong, yet even in its most powerful stages, nylon chew bones such as the Nylabone® chew products can successfully guide this potentially destructive tendency into a physically and psychologically beneficial act. Chew bones are good for your dog's teeth and help vent anxieties that may otherwise disturb your dog.

This group of healthy pups is about to take a ride. When traveling, as with any time when your dog is in his crate, it is important not to allow the duration of time to become prolonged. This is an invitation to soil the crate and thereby becomes a setback to the housebreaking process.

meet the needs of the puppy. Such a schedule should be rigid if it is to be effective. Owners can bend such a schedule if necessary as long as they realize that any change will lengthen the time needed for housebreaking. Make a schedule and keep it.

If an owner is at home throughout the day, then the day can begin at (let us say) 7:00 AM by taking the puppy out of its crate for a walk. This should be followed by a 15-minute meal at 7:30 AM and another walk at 7:45 AM. The puppy should then be allowed to play on a tiled or linoleum floor for a quarter hour before once again being locked in the crate. At noon, the puppy should be taken for another walk and allowed another 15 minutes of playtime before being placed in the crate again. At 4:00 PM this routine should be repeated: walk, play, and confinement. At 7:00 PM, the routine is repeated again. At 11:00 PM, a final walk should be taken before overnight confinement.

For working owners, the schedule has to be altered by walking the puppy first thing in the morning, feeding it, and allowing it playtime while the owners are getting ready to leave. An additional quick walk right before leaving for the day is recommended. The puppy should then be confined in the crate until the owners return in the evening. Upon returning, they should immediately walk the puppy for about 20 minutes be-

Alternative Methods

fore feeding it. After eating, the puppy should be walked again and allowed another 20-minute play activity on a tiled or linoleum floor. Another walk should follow before the puppy is put into the crate. Around 11:00 PM a final walk should be taken—right before putting the puppy in its crate for the night.

The "home" schedule designed for a puppy who is at home with someone all day is far easier on the animal, of course. However, today's somewhat frantic work schedules do not always allow such a luxury. The working owner's schedule is probably the more common simply by necessity. It might be a wise suggestion to hire someone—perhaps a neighbor—to come in and maintain the home schedule. If this is not practical, the owner should not worry. The puppy will be able to adapt to any schedule as long as it is maintained for a length of time.

Homeowners who can afford a pen can, if they desire, eliminate the need for walking the dog once and for all. If a pen is contructed next to a door with a dog port, the dog may enter

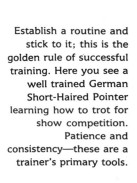

Establish a routine and stick to it; this is the golden rule of successful training. Here you see a well trained German Short-Haired Pointer learning how to trot for show competition. Patience and consistency—these are a trainer's primary tools.

This metal structure can serve two functions; indoors it can be used as a housebreaking crate, or, outdoors it can be used as a temporary pen (as illustrated in the photo). Note that this enclosure does not have a top; some dog enthusiasts of today feel that a lid may be detrimental to the dog's psyche.

Obedience is to respect as affection is to kindness, and respect is to affection as kindness is to love. This little Mastiff pup will some day weigh in excess of 150 pounds; obedience will be of utmost importance. Here this young pup is receiving the mellowing ingredient of kindness as he plays with his master.

Alternative Methods

In the photo to the right is a dog, kept in a pen, with access to the indoors or outdoors through a dog-port. Such pen-with-port structures are beneficial for the owner who may not be around enough to let his dog out several times during the day. Contrary to some practices, a dog-port does not eliminate the need to walk your dog on a regular basis. In the lower photo are shown two dogs being walked as easily as one. Your local pet store will have an adaptation that will enable this to be done, provided that the dogs are equally well-trained.

All are of the same litter, all have similar markings, all will experience similar situations while in the early care of their mother; yet, each will grow to be an individual, no two will be entirely the same. Each will require some slight difference in training.

and leave whenever it wants. Various pens and ready-made dog ports are available. Training the dog to enter and leave through a dog port should not be difficult. The swinging hinge type of port can be tied or propped open, allowing the dog to clearly see the outside pen. Coaxing the dog through the door with food and praising it each time it goes through the dog port door will encourage it to use the opening on its own in a very short time. As the days go by, the door can be lowered so that the opening becomes smaller. Finally, the port will be closed completely, but by then the dog will have already learned to nuzzle its way through.

Every puppy and every owner are individuals. No recommended schedule will be perfect for all owners and all puppies. Adjustments will have to be made in each and every case. Sometimes a puppy can go an hour or more before needing to go out. Some can only "hold it in" a few minutes. Whatever the case, alter the schedule to meet the puppy's needs. Walk it when needed or let it have playtime when it appears most active. A compromise between the puppy's natural schedule and the owner's daily schedule will lead to the best timing of housebreaking activity.

Alternative Methods

If a puppy does not go during its scheduled walk, then it should be put back in the crate until the next scheduled walk time to reinforce what a walk is all about. The puppy will soil its crate only if it has just been introduced to it and does not yet realize that it will be closed in with the mess for a long time or if the crate is too large for the puppy. If the crate is the scene of an accident, the puppy should be scolded and immediately taken for a walk. It is likely that it will go again once outside. If so, praise the animal and then bring it back to the crate. The crate must be completely cleaned before the dog is once again

"All gone? No more?" Many a pup's eyes are bigger than his stomach. Remember that a puppy's system can only handle a small meal and should be fed several times a day, rather than the traditional once-a-day meal served to fully grown dogs. Sometimes it is more a case of a pup's desire to chew than his need to eat; therefore, it is a good idea to have available for your pup a safe and effective chew-product.

confined. Keeping the animal in a dirty crate will only serve to allow the puppy to become used to filthy surroundings. This is exactly the opposite of what is meant to be accomplished by housebreaking. The goal is to make the dog absolutely hate being dirty. After discovering an accident, always clean the crate as soon as possible.

If the puppy is about to go, it will give signals. Careful observation on the part of the owner will allow these signs to be recognized and the puppy to be taken out as soon as needed. Most of the time, when the urge to go comes upon the puppy, it will stop whatever it has been doing and take on a look of intense concentration. Slightly older puppies will sometimes begin to circle; this may be difficult in the confinement of a training crate, but they'll manage it. When the owner spots these motions, he should carefully and calmly lift the puppy out of the crate and take it for a walk. Owners are cautioned against rushing toward the animal in a frenzied attempt to get it outside before it's too late. Such movement will only scare the animal into having the very accident that the owner is trying to prevent.

Soon, the reasons for this routine will dawn on the puppy and it will begin to deposit wastes outside as a matter of course. The puppy will endeavor to keep its crate dry. When this becomes apparent, then walks and playtime can be extended. However, don't over-anticipate the puppy's progress. If the owner begins to regularly extend the time the puppy is freed from the crate before the animal is ready, it will only prolong housebreaking training. The puppy can gradually spend its free time in other areas of the house. As time goes by (a few months, at least) it can be left alone in different areas of the house for five or ten minutes. There *will* be mistakes on the part of the dog. There has never been a dog that has completely understood the housebreaking routine right from the start. As long as scolding is administered properly, the animal will understand and learn from its mistakes.

Some extremely small breeds of dog may never want to venture outside, by their own choice or by the choice of their owners. If this is the case, the owner may want to only paper train the puppy and never teach it to use anything else. It is suggested, however, that very small dogs may be neater companions if they are trained, like cats, to use a litter box. These boxes, available at pet shops, can be placed in an area the dog frequents and which is easy to get to and keep clean. The bottom of these boxes may be lined with newspapers (if the puppy has been previously paper trained) or with conventional litter.

Training with the litter box is done exactly like paper training, beginning with confining the puppy to an area containing only the box and a place to sleep. Hopefully, the puppy will realize right away which area is for which activity. If it is confused, it should be sternly corrected until it understands.

Puppies need a lot of sleep; they tire easily; their play-time should not be extended to the point of fatigue. When exercising your puppy, watch carefully for signs of tiredness. Such a yawn as the one expelled by this lovely little pup could mean that it's time for a nap.

The sleeping area can be slowly enlarged to include a play area. Eventually the animal can have freedom throughout the entire house. It will seek out the litter box to deposit its wastes no matter where in the house the box is located. The box can also be placed in an out-of-the-way area and the dog can be led to it at an appropriate time, such as when it awakens or after a short walk. This will help train the animal to use the box at certain times of the day. As in the case of all other housebreaking methods, the dog should be praised when it uses the box and scolded when it misses or forgets.

Separation Anxiety

A major obstacle in any dog training can be overcome if separation anxiety is eliminated early on. Dogs are highly sociable animals that require a very strong and continual attachment to their own kind. If this is unavailable, they quite naturally transfer this inbred need to their human caretakers. When a puppy arrives at its new home, it has usually just been weaned from its mother. Even at the young age of two or three months, the puppy is getting used to long periods of time away from its mother; it is beginning to take these absences for granted, but still requires companionship. Luckily, its owner is usually more than willing to provide that needed comfort.

Still, there is a period of adjustment. Just after being brought to its new home, a puppy may cry for great amounts of time. It should not take too long for this to subside. Once the puppy becomes used to its new surroundings and once it realizes that its crying is not going to bring about any change, its crying will decrease and will soon stop altogether.

Many dog owners have shortened this period of adjustment by placing a loud ticking clock and a hot water bottle near the puppy to simulate the heartbeat and warmth of its mother. The repetitive noise of the clock and the warmth of the hot water bottle have a calming effect on the animal. In recent times, some owners have been using the electronic "hearts" in some toy teddy bears to simulate the heartbeat of the puppy's mother.

FACING PAGE: During the early weeks (or even months) of their lives, puppies are rarely alone. Because of this, they may develop anxiety when first separated from their mates. Do not fret, though, for pups soon find that your love and affection compensate for what they have lost.

There are many dog owners who cannot stand a puppy's crying for more than a couple of nights. They report that they soon bring the puppy into their bedroom and let it sleep in or near their bed to provide the necessary companionship. In regard to housebreaking, nothing could be more destructive. The puppy must be made to realize that it is the owner who makes the rules in the house. Even a young puppy can sense a pattern if its owner begins to bend to the puppy's desires. This is the exact opposite of the action which is required for proper housebreaking. Although it may seem cruel, the owner's motto should be, "Let it cry."

Along with separation anxiety and anxiety-related urinating and defecating (often diarrhea), the puppy may also vomit and exhibit tendencies to chew and/or dig. It may also stop eating and drinking if it is overwrought because of being separated from its mother or its owner. This kind of behavior usually occurs about five or ten minutes after the dog finds itself alone. If these actions have been allowed to continue for a time, they may even take place prior to the dog's being left

Who will be the first to go? The big guy coming over the corner seems to be the most willing, yet, despite his eagerness, he too may suffer some anxiety when first separated from his kin.

Yearning for his master's return. This candid shot reveals the loneliness that dogs often experience due to being left to themselves for a long period of the day. Consider your available time before deciding on a dog as a pet.

alone. Dogs are very observant and easily become used to routine. If the owner leaves at the same time every day, the dog's internal system will alert it as to when to expect to be alone. The same holds true if the dog sees its owner pick up a brief case or go through any other routine that signals departure. The dog knows that separation is coming and will quickly be overcome with anxiety.

"Happy that you're home." Many dogs like to offer family members a gift upon their return to the home; often, as is the case with this young pup, it is a favorite toy or play-towel.

Separation Anxiety

Play-time is over and a certain sense of resistance is seen in this Mastiff pup's eyes as he attempts to hide himself in the lawn. Playing with your pup is an excellent way to build a lasting bond between the two of you, and although stamina is minimal during early puppyhood, adequate play-time is essential to the pup's well being and successful compliance with desired training. Between the pup's desire and your available time, a mutually agreeable play schedule should be easily established.

A gradual increase in separation time will get the puppy used to being alone for longer and longer periods of time. Start by leaving the puppy alone for a few minutes at a time. Gradually build up to longer periods of time. If the puppy is confined in a room, the owner will not have to leave the house. Simply leave the room for a few minutes, making the puppy believe that it is alone.

Potential puppy owners should take into consideration their time spent away from home before getting a puppy. If they are going to be out of the house for ten hours a day, then they had better arrange for somone to look after the puppy for part of that time, or they should decide on another kind of pet. A puppy cannot stand to be left alone for so long a period of

time. The lack of social companionship will have serious future consequences that will make housebreaking (and any additional training) very, very difficult and frustrating. While confinement to a room or a crate is the way recommended by most experts to accomplish housebreaking, they all agree that the periods of time in which the puppy is alone must be counterbalanced by companionship the rest of the time. Balance is the key word.

These two photographs illustrate the mutually gentle playfulness of both people and dogs. Perhaps this quality is one of the keys to the harmonious compatibility of man and dog.

Traveling

If a housebroken dog has to travel, certain considerations have to be remembered. Traveling in a car is really no problem as long as there are frequent rest stops along the route where the dog can be taken out for a walk. The animal should be leashed while in the car, with the leash looped around some safe point of attachment. *Never* leash the dog to anything attached to the door, as it could be roughly pulled when someone exits. Having the leash already on the dog's collar eliminates any delay in hooking it on when the car stops. The owner should also carry with him a pooper-scooper and some plastic bags in the event that the local laws require the cleanup of dog waste. It's always best to be prepared. In addition, a quantity of drinking water should be brought along for the dog just in case water facilities are not available at rest stops.

It is suggested that a few old towels be kept in the car in case the dog gets sick. Dogs vomit much more easily than human beings. Nervousness and motion sickness often overcome traveling dogs, even those that are used to riding in a car. Sometimes the animal will get sick during a short trip to the veterinarian or to the corner store. However, dogs do show signs before they get sick, and an alert owner can sometimes get the animal out of the car before it has a chance to make a mess. Before vomiting, the dog will begin rapidly panting and salivating. On a prolonged journey, the dog should be fed four hours before departure. Since there is more of a rocking motion on the floor of the car than on the seat, try to keep the dog on

FACING PAGE: This is not the recommended way to travel with your dog(s). Traveling in this manner can be hazardous to yourself and to your pet. When you travel and bring your dog along, it is best to place him in a proper and adequate crate designed for such purposes.

Most dogs, including this Bully, enjoy car travel if they are introduced to it at an early age. This photo demonstrates one of the many hazards of driving with an un-crated dog; without warning, he can move to the driver's side of the car and obstruct vision.

the seat as much as possible. These precautions will both cut down on the number of rest stops and lessen the occurrences of car sickness. Never give a dog tranquilizers to calm it down for a trip unless they have been recommended by a veterinarian.

Another major caution must be made regarding dogs in cars. It must be remembered that dogs do not sweat in the same manner as humans. They eliminate their body heat by panting. The heat is released through the animal's tongue. While the dog is panting, it salivates, producing extra moisture. When this moisture evaporates in the dog's mouth, the animal's blood is cooled; this, in turn, cools down the dog's entire body temperature. If, for some reason, the dog is unable to pant enough to cool itself down, its temperature will rapidly rise and it will fall victim to what is known as heat prostration.

The symptoms of heat prostration include the dog's struggling to breath. In addition, its eyes will appear glazed and there may be a bit of foaming at the mouth. Vomiting may occur. The dog will pace or exhibit other frantic movements. Naturally, its temperature will soar. In the final stages of heat prostration, a dog's gums will turn pale or blue. Convulsions, coma, and death will follow rapidly thereafter.

The major cause of heat prostration in dogs is *leaving them alone in closed automobiles.* In the warm summer

These two pictures demonstrate the correct and the incorrect way to travel with your dog. In the photo to the left you see two dogs projecting their heads out of a car window. This is especially hazardous to your pets' eyes, as objects can easily fly into them and cause severe damage. In the photo to the right you see a car that has been prepared to safely transport canines.

months, the temperature in a closed car parked in the sun can climb to 150° in a matter of minutes. Under *no* circumstances should a dog be left in a closed car for *any* amount of time.

Bus, plane, and train travel all have varying degrees of regulation concerning animal transportation. Most of these forms of travel require that a dog be confined to a crate. Rest stops on a bus trip may be possible, but no such opportunities present themselves on trains or planes. If a dog must use either of these last two modes of transportation, the best thing their owners can do for them is to feed them four hours prior to their boarding the train or plane.

Puppies tire easily; they can become fatigued, stressed, or even sick if they are subjected to long bouts of work, play, or even traveling. Because of this, it is not recommended that you take your young pup on prolonged journeys unless absolutely necessary.

There are a number of common errors that novice owners make when attempting to housebreak their puppy. While some may have been covered elsewhere, they are mentioned here as a general checklist to remember.

Possible

Problems

Puppies should not be fed too late at night. Larger or older dogs' systems will take a full twelve hours to completely digest food. The time for smaller dogs or puppies is considerably less, sometimes as short as six to eight hours. Water seems to go through a dog's system immediately. Owners are cautioned to calculate when to conveniently feed their dogs.

Laxity in scheduling is why many early attempts at housebreaking fail. Even the youngest puppy can quickly adapt to a schedule; even faster can they forget a schedule that is not maintained.

How does a dog owner know if housebreaking has been accomplished? When can the dog owner return to his own schedule without worrying about his home being messed up by the dog when it is left alone?

The only way to determine if housebreaking has been successful is for the owner to make sure that certain things *never* occur. If for any reason *whatsoever* the dog urinates or defecates in the house, it is *not* housebroken. It doesn't matter if the weather is bad or the dog simply "forgot"; if it happens, then the housebreaking routine has to be strictly maintained. If the dog is any younger than six or seven months old, then

FACING PAGE: One of the most common ailments troubling dogs today is skin problems, especially those caused by fleas and ticks. In addition to sprays and powders, a good bath will help prevent many such disorders.

housebreaking has simply not been completed. If the dog is any older, then there could very well be a problem with the animal.

The older dog who displays unhousebroken tendencies must not be allowed to get away with such behavior. This type of dog is busy taking over the house and claiming it as its own territory. It considers itself the master of the house. Experts feel that the only way to train such an animal is to use the crate method (from scratch), just as if the animal were still a puppy. The re-training will take just as long as it would have when the animal was a puppy. There should be no rush on the part of the owner to once again allow the dog to have free run of the house. The dog will very likely "complain" via a few nights of barking, but it will eventually accept its fate and take to the re-training. The owner must not be swayed by the dog's pitiful displays. Running a fan near the dog's crate during the night will help keep the agitated animal cool and also help to drown out barking noise. Quite literally, the dog owner is putting up a battle for his or her house.

Under these circumstances, it may be necessary to accentuate scolding to an exaggerated degree. If the dog does soil the house, the owner should overreact when finding the mess. The dog should be taken by the collar and firmly shaken, lifting

Travel crates for dogs come in many sizes and colors; they are perhaps the best way to prevent unnecessary injury from coming to your dog. Be sure that both the crate and the car are well ventilated. Never leave your dog alone in a parked car, especially in the summer, as heat prostration can quickly kill your pet.

When correcting your dog, be firm. It is a good idea to accentuate your tone to emphasize your intention. Never use confusing commands and always be consistent in your laying down of the rules.

the forepaws off the floor, putting all of its weight on the hind legs. At the accident site, a stern and firm tone of voice should be used to say such things as "Bad dog" and "Shame." The dog should then be taken for a walk. When returning to the house, the scolding should be repeated as if the accident had been discovered for the first time. The dog should then be returned to its crate, confined, and ignored. The soiled area should then be completely cleaned or else the dog will think it can go there again.

Another consideration is whether or not the owner has had a dog living in the house previously. If so, the scent of this previous occupant has to be totally removed before introducing the new dog into the environment. The house has to be odorfree. A dog's nose is so powerful that it can detect one part urine to a million parts water. Normal household deodorants and ammonia may hide the odor from humans, but not from dogs. The cleaning of "spots" has to be done thoroughly. The dog owner may have to investigate the possibility of obtaining industrial strength cleaning agents that are specially designed to clean up after dogs.

With some overly aggressive dogs, a firm tone of voice may not be enough to teach them that the owner means business. This may be more of a problem when re-training an older dog. These animals have become used to their owner's voice and may know, deep down, that the owner doesn't really mean what his tone of voice seems to indicate. For such dogs, a device known as a "shake-can" is a valuable tool. The shake-can is nothing more than an empty soda can filled about halfway with pennies or pebbles. The sound that is made when shaking the pennies or pebbles in the can is frightening to a dog. Shaking the can at the dog as a scolding can be very effective. The dog will comply with what the owner desires in an effort to prevent hearing the disturbing rattling sound.

Submissive urination is a common problem that is easily overcome. This type of accident occurs when the pet excitedly greets its owner after a separation and it dribbles urine. This may happen while the dog is standing and wagging its tail or rolling over on its back. In the strict sense, a dog that has this problem may still be considered to be housbroken. This is really a case of overreaction to a particular person or situation. It is the dog's way of acknowledging that the owner is still in charge.

The way to correct this problem is to tone down homecomings. When the owner returns home the dog should be gently petted and no roughhousing should take place. If the dog is made to believe that homecoming is no big deal, it will soon treat such occurrences more casually.

Marking their territory with urine is a characteristic of many dogs; such behavior is usually more common in males than in females. The male dog will lift its leg and deposit a tiny amount of urine in many locations around the house. It may also choose objects that are new to the house. This habit manifests itself after the male has reached sexual maturity. While it can certainly be "trained out" of the dog by a good housebreaking method, it is often totally eliminated by neutering or castrating.

Feeding is a very important factor in housebreaking.

In his overzealous desire to greet his homecoming master, this virile young Beagle is climbing out of his pen, potentially causing injury to himself and setting a poor example for his mates to follow. If you have such an overreacting greeter, follow this text and tone down homecomings.

After all, this is the input that leads to the output which housebreaking is all about. If an owner wants his or her dog to have proper housebreaking habits, then proper feeding habits have to be established. The sooner an eating schedule is set up, the better for the dog *and* the owner. At a very early age, the puppy should be weaned to a good commercial dog food. If this is done and the dog becomes used to this diet early, then it won't be demanding table scraps. In fact, dog owners should always discourage children and visitors from offering the dog table scraps or other mealtime treats. This is extremely important during housebreaking and should be a standing rule. Beyond destroying the animal's daily schedule, eating a possibly unbalanced volume of food could lead to ailments. These could be dangerous at worst and annoying (especially when housebreaking) at best.

Sometimes illness can cause a dog to have an accident. The owner may be inclined to overlook this infraction of the rules because the animal is sick, but this is not recommended. Scolding must be carried out even if the dog is ill. A thoroughly housebroken dog would rather lay down and die before it would relieve itself in the house. A trained dog who is sick will be completely mortified if it soils the house. It will, most likely,

Even when a dog is not feeling well, the rules of the house must be kept, and although scolding may be toned down, correction is imperative.

whine, cry, and slink away in shame. Even so, the owner must scold the animal, mildly, by taking it to the spot and saying "Bad dog, shame." Since the dog is ill, there should be no shaking or loud tone of voice, but the animal must be reminded that under *no circumstances* is this kind of behavior permitted in the house. After this happens, the owner will have to realize that a

For one reason or another your dog may become ill. It is wise to have a general knowledge of dog ailments prior to such a dilemma. There are some fine books on this subject available today.

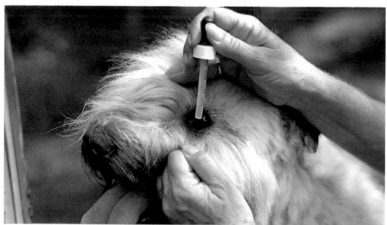

closer watch for signs of the dog's needs will have to be maintained.

Owners should always be on the lookout for certain medical problems which may hinder housebreaking. If a dog owner notices that his pet is reluctant to defecate or observes it sliding along the ground on its rear end, these actions may be symptoms of a problem with the animal's anal glands. These glands, found on either side of the dog's rectum, are closely related to the dog's bodily functions in this area. The anal gland is actually a territorial marking tool utilized by most wild animals. However, in most breeds of domesticated dogs, this scent gland no longer has any true purpose.

There are far too many hazardous objects for your dog to chew on for you not to provide him with a safe nylon bone.

Scent is constantly produced by the glandular tissue. If the narrow neck does become clogged, the gland will become filled with its own secretion. Eventually, this will cause a rupture beneath the skin since the secreted liquid cannot escape. If the owner detects soreness and inflammation in the dog's anal area, and if the dog is constantly licking and biting its rear (along with the dog's reluctance to defecate and its sliding along the floor), a veterinarian should be consulted. Fortunately, the gland can be surgically removed if it is a constant problem and if the veterinarian recommends its removal. There are no ill effects suffered by the dog if such an operation is necessary.

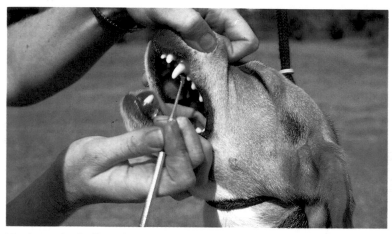

Like human's, dog's teeth too can accumulate plaque and tartar. Nylon chew bones are often enough to prevent this, but if your dog develops a problem spot, it is best to have it removed by a professional, for a build-up can cause gum disease.

Chronic prostate trouble and hernias can show up in male dogs. The prostate may be the problem if the dog is seen straining to urinate. A hernia appears as a soft lump in the rear end or the groin area. These conditions, if detected, should be examined by a vet as soon as possible.

If, for no apparent reason, a dog becomes unhousebroken, the owner should observe whether or not the dog has begun to drink an unusually large amount of water. If this is the case, the dog may be suffering from a kidney disorder. Owners should continue to give the dog as much water as it needs since it is attempting to make up for the work the kidney is no longer performing. It may be necessary to take the animal for more extended walks. As with any medical problem in pets, a veterinarian should be consulted as soon as possible.

Another medical problem that may cause difficulties in housebreaking is urinary tract stones. In canines, these stones normally develop in the bladder, but have been found in almost every area of a dog's urinary tract. They have been known to appear singly or in many different areas of the urinary tract at the same time. They can be found in one or both kidneys or in the ureter after they have been passed from the kidneys.

The actual cause of these stones is unknown, but infection in the urinary tract, blockage of urine overflow, diet,

Possible Problems

and heredity are all considered factors in different cases. Frequent urination, straining to urinate, or complete blockage of urination are all possible signs of urinary tract stones. A veterinarian should be consulted without delay.

Trauma to the urinary tract or cancer of the bladder may also cause problems in housebreaking. Aging can have a serious effect on an animal's ability to control its bodily functions. Dogs suffering from constipation may also present housebreaking problems. If blood is noted in the dog's urine, if the dog is straining to defecate, or if there is an unusual discharge from the rectum, the dog should be examined by a veterinarian as soon as possible.

Almost all dog experts suggest that frequent examinations be performed on pet dogs by their owners. Check for soreness or irritation of the ears, eyes, nose, mouth, feet, and tail.

Remember, a sick dog will not respond to training of any kind except with frustration and ultimate disappointment for both itself and its owner.

Worms can complicate the housebreaking process. A pup can get worms from a dormant egg in the mother's nipple. All pups should have the proper shots from a veterinarian.

The Lasting Bond

Although it is commonly believed that young puppies are unable to learn much beyond the sound of their own name, recent studies indicate that these young dogs are very responsive to their environments and are eager to explore their surroundings. Although most dog-training institutions will not accept puppies unless they are at least six months old, there are indications that the dogs are willing and able to learn at a younger age.

A puppy's desire to learn about its surroundings and its initial curiosity is set at a crucial period sometime between eight and 12 weeks of age. Research shows that if there is no interactive handling or simple training during this period, the puppy will have a lower intelligence quotient when it reaches adulthood. Simple play makes for a strong foundation for housebreaking and other training later in the puppy's life. Many people who have complained that their training efforts did not produce the desired results have confessed that they delayed any training attempts until after this critical time in their puppy's life.

No matter how early they are introduced to people, puppies of this age will still experience moments of fear. A gentle and warm interaction with the puppy is paramount. The more social experiences the puppy has, the faster the fear will fade away. The faster fear fades, the quicker trust is established. The quicker trust is established, the faster the dog and owner can get on to the task of housebreaking and training and

FACING PAGE: The lasting bond of happiness and love is achieved in no other person-to-pet relationship as it is between the human and the dog. It is seen no more clearly than in the sparkling eyes of a child who is accompanied by his faithful friend.

the pleasures of their lifelong companionship.

Children love to imitate their parents. They are often observed "taking care" of their dolls in the exact same manner as their parents treat them. Being able to transfer this love to a living creature such as a puppy has the potential of being the greatest experience a young child can have. With a careful, guiding parental hand, caring for and housebreaking a puppy can teach a child much about the *human* experience. If the child is fortunate enough to have seen the puppy develop from its first day, this awe and wonder can be enriched each day as they learn together.

This odyssey of learning will not replace the parents' responsibility. No matter how interested the child may be in the training of the dog, the parents will still have the major burden of walking, praising, and scolding the animal. The important thing for the parents to remember is to teach the child to use the same commands and the same tones of voice which they use toward the dog. The dog will learn only if all is consistent. Depending on the age of the child, he or she may not be able to clean up after an accident or even walk the dog. However, the link between the dog and the child can be established if the child is involved in all of the housebreaking activities, even if it is only standing by and watching as the parent trains the dog. The child will learn by watching and the dog will come to recognize the child's presence during the training period. Eventually, the child will learn (i.e., be trained) to care for the animal by himself or herself. If the initial excitement about owning a pet has been maintained, this transfer of responsibilities will be a great goal to reach—for the child, the parents, and the pet.

The following books by T.F.H. publications are available at pet shops everywhere.

SUGGESTED READING

ATLAS OF DOG BREEDS OF THE WORLD By Bonnie Wilcox, DVM, and Chris Walkowicz (H-1091)

Traces the history and highlights the characteristics, appearances and functions of every recognized dog breed from the four corners of the world. Over 400 different breeds are covered, and every breed is shown in full color. Hundreds of breeds in addition to those recognized by the AKC and The Kennel Club of Great Britain are included—flock guards, mastiffs, gun dogs, scenthounds, herding dogs, terriers, northern and southern breeds—they are all here and they are all interesting.

Hard cover, 9" x 12", over 900 pages
Contains over 1000 full-color photos.

T.F.H. ALL (160) BREED DOG GROOMING By a Panel of Experts (H-1095)

How to groom all the breeds recognized by the AKC and the Kennel Club of Great Britain. Includes general information about bathing, dematting, cleaning the ears, equipment needed, and many other topics in addition to providing specific step-by-step grooming instructions for each breed. Fully illustrated throughout with full-color drawings and photographs, this convenient spiral-bound edition allows groomers to have step-by-step instructions at their fingertips. For all professional dog groomers, veterans and beginners alike.

Spiral bound, 8½" x 11", 272 pp.

DOG TRAINING by Lew Burke (H-962)

For dog owners age 14 and up who are anxious to discover the secrets behind Lew Burke's methods. The elements of dog training are easy to grasp and apply. The author uses the psychological makeup of dogs to his advantage by making them want to be what they should be—substituting the family for the pack.

Hard cover, 5½" x 8", 255 pp.
64 black and white photos, 23 color photos

Index